Love, Loss and Transfiguration

Dedication

I am deeply honored, grateful and humbled to have loved, and been loved by some of the most incredible people ever to take breath on this planet. I mean love in its most complete range of expression: romantic, platonic, familial, spiritual, universal and the myriad other forms it manifests. When I look back at the journey through this gift called life, it is the love I hold for you all that will be my greatest treasure. For those lost to time, geography, mortality or whatever, that same love is also my greatest solace.

The words and images in this book were born of love too. You have laughed with me, cried with me, held me, and nurtured me. You have stolen my heart, broken it utterly and you have healed it too. We have adventured together, played together and grown together. You have saved both my figurative and literal life on so many occasions. More than you know if truth be told. Through it all we have changed. I like to believe we have evolved.

There is often sorrow in the words I write and the images I make, but so too is there joy and pure exuberant pleasure. This world we share is a marvel beyond imagining and there is beauty in even the darkest places. I hope you will find beauty here too. For you. This book is for you.

With Love
-Dale R Cody

Fall in Love With Your Life

What I Believe

Fall in love with your life. Court it. Romance it. Learn to lead and take it dancing in the far corners of the world and your imagination. Dine with it and savor all the tastes in all the places you can. Eat burgers, bouillabaisse, toasted crickets, pad thai, shawarma, couscous, rich dark chocolate, coffee, and a million other tasty delights right in the places where they live. Eat from street vendors and five-star restaurants; feeling the love and care that each chef puts into their work. Picnic in the park and spill red wine on fine white tablecloths where uniformed waiters slide around fancy tables in dimly lit venues. Throw morsels into the air and watch seagulls catch them, while suspended on invisible currents of air.

Fall in love with your life. Ask it out and when it says yes, treat it like the treasure it is. Get to know it by being with it. By really, truly being with it. Ask deep probing questions of it and see what lies beneath its surface. Float gently with it on calm sunny days and sail it too, when the storms blow hard and the waves crash like hammer blows across the bow. Keep it afloat and in good repair. Sail it into the endless fjords, inlets and rivers, but most of all, take it across the oceans and meet the world with it. Dock it for an hour, a day, or a month in some distant harbor and get to know the people there. They will enrich your life and teach you things about it you would never otherwise discover. You will see them in the mirror every-time you look, and then love them all the more.

Fall in love with your life. Massage its feet with the oil of travel. Caress them with the endless paths and places they yearn to visit. Love them with use rather than idleness and stupor. Strengthen your love with exercise, discipline and experience. Treat it as you would any muscle or thoroughbred, by employing it in vigorous activity, in fresh air, under kaleidoscopic skies.

Fall in love with your life. You must be a participant in it and not simply a spectator. Get in the driver's seat and road test it. Every day. Be a creator rather than a consumer. Let the world inspire you and then make something. Paint. Draw. Write. Make images instead of taking pictures. Give rather than take. Be a designer. Design your life consciously and with deliberate purpose.

Write the grand story of your life and live it like the best book you've ever read. You are not simply the author, but also the protagonist in this narrative, so craft your tale with love and care and richness of detail. You cannot change the pages behind you, so do not try. Accept them if you cannot embrace them and use them as background for the next chapters. Share the book of your life with others and read theirs as well. Learn as well as teach. Inspire and be inspired.

Fall in love with your life. Grow older with it, but never grow old. See and experience the world with the eyes of a child, even when your skin sags and age tries to bend you. Do not genuflect at this alter of time. Keep your thoughts and actions from ossifying, by loving and living your life full out. Make it your first love and your last. No one can love your life the way you can, and in so loving it, you are more able to love others. You are also more able to let them love you. This is the real reward for falling in love with your life.

Fall in love with your life and it will fall in love with you.

AUG

•

The First Artist

- In Loving Memory of Mervin J Cody from Your Children

You saw me take my first breath

As I witnessed your last

Your hands held mine

In the beginning

And I your's

At the end

Shepherding one another

In that transition

From one plane to the next

Guardian and guide

And in between

Those countless breaths

Innumerable steps

Your wisdom

A profound empathy for all living things

Unparalled generosity and selflessness

Born aloft on wings of pure love

Flying on the currents of time

Joy, sorrow, laughter and memory

Countless moments from the books of life

A shared experience

As I am part of you

So too, do you live in me

I am a canvas

Where lives the exertions of a lifetime

Your opus perhaps

If I am your gift to the future

Then I pray be a grand gift indeed

I pray I do not disappoint

You gave everything for your creation

Could I possibly do less?

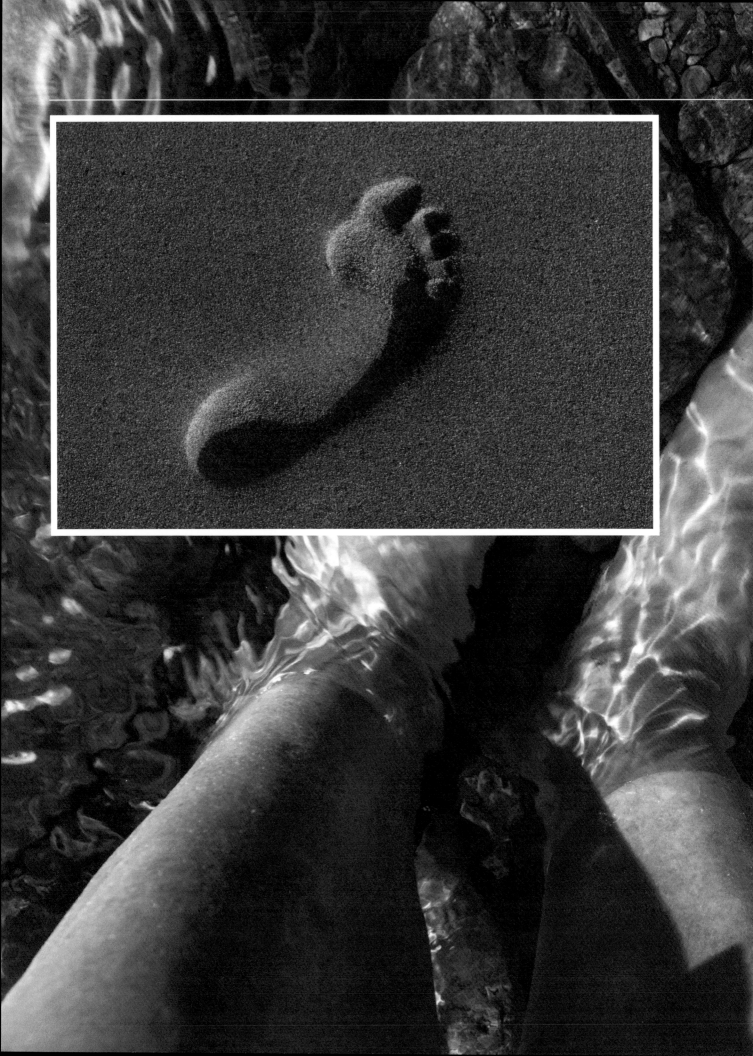

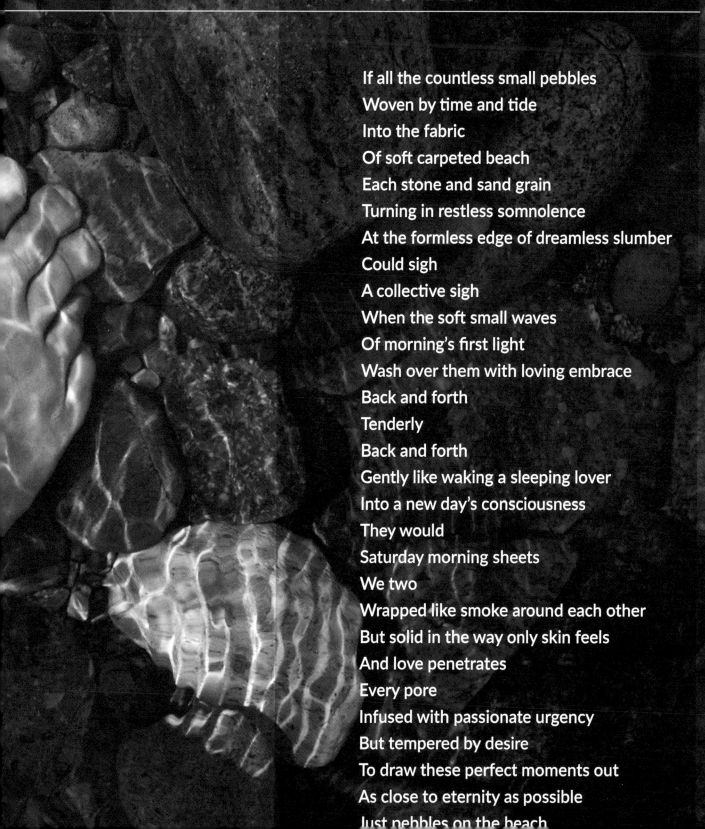

We Two

If all the countless small pebbles
Woven by time and tide
Into the fabric
Of soft carpeted beach
Each stone and sand grain
Turning in restless somnolence
At the formless edge of dreamless slumber
Could sigh
A collective sigh
When the soft small waves
Of morning's first light
Wash over them with loving embrace
Back and forth
Tenderly
Back and forth
Gently like waking a sleeping lover
Into a new day's consciousness
They would
Saturday morning sheets
We two
Wrapped like smoke around each other
But solid in the way only skin feels
And love penetrates
Every pore
Infused with passionate urgency
But tempered by desire
To draw these perfect moments out
As close to eternity as possible
Just pebbles on the beach

Dark Places

There is beauty to be found in the dark places too. Set aside expectations and preconceptions to seek it out. It's there in the shadows and under rocks where you might not think to look. There is beauty in truth, but not always truth in beauty.

Thistles

Find sunshine through the thistles
There is beauty and small miracles
Everywhere you look...

Dream

Let me trace once more
With fingers real
Those perfect places
That sigh with my touch
Push back that lush ochre and gold curtain
A cascade waterfall
Let me kiss again
With lips and teeth and tongue
That delicate apricot yum
A hidden treasure beneath
As simple as an ear
As complex a gateway as ever to be found
As magnificent as any temple conceived
Bas relief sculptural beauty in contrast
Velvet smooth curves
And a golden harvest of tiny corn silk hair
Stopped in their silent march
From nape to blade
And beyond

Impossibly, indescribably smooth
A landscape no human artist could duplicate
No critic
No eye
No sense
Could deny

Powerful currents of energy pulse unseen
Electric finger touch giving and taking
The stuff of life and the stuff beyond it

Flower for me again
that verdant meadow
Lush with color, perfume and soft curving shapes
Heavy with the morning dew
Ripe with promise, passion and new life
A canvas upon which to create
A masterpiece
Where desire lays down brushstrokes
And senses mix
Like colors on a palette
Crazy, powerful, subtle and sublime
Did I paint there once before
My opus

And still fall short?
Bring back the summer sun
The taste of you on me
When our lips met
In sensual caress
Passionate, gentle, still urgent
Tongues softly stir the mix
Those flavors of love, lust and tender emotion

Etched in my memory
The sole lithograph on gallery walls
The way Klimt depicts two lovers
Entwined patterns of color, flesh and texture
A palpable love and yet a mystery

Would that I could paint again
Upon that glorious dream

Among Giants

Lay with me among giants
On a mattress made of needles
Gaze at the heavens
Arms for trunks
Hands for canopies
And fingers
Move soft with the breeze

Trace clouds like actors
Making dreams in the sky
Making us believe
In dragons, faeries, windmills, giants
And magic
Each other
Breathe the sky with me my love
Breathe the sky

The Dreaming Library

Meet me in the library of dreams
My Love
Meet me as we sleep
Embrace me at the counter
And feel the delicate sweet taste
Of your lips on mine
Let us begin the journey there
Among the places, thoughts and imagination
Sleeping dormant on their shelves

Each one a nascent adventure
Awaiting discovery
Requiring only solution or catalyst

Desire

A reagent for exploration
And possibility
If you write me into your book
I will pen you into mine

We will write each verse together
Born on the voyages we make
And the steps we take
At the end you will loan me your book
I will lend you mine

In study and perusal we will find
Each other
And ourselves

In what guise did first we meet?
And what took so long
For reunion in this one?
Past mid-day, but well before the sundown
Still agonizingly late
In what castle, hovel or manse
Beside which riverbank
And under what warm liquid sun
Have we danced and played
Laughed and made love?

Before

What sandstone caverns
Have we yet to explore
Together
Hands and fingers twined
The way roots wind around each other
In the earth
Bare feet tread softly, carefully
Along the warm 60 grit floor
Into and out of tepid pools
Pearls dotted along the way
Worn well through red rock canals
Into a perfect winding path

Through patterned camouflage
Of sun and shadow
To the sanctuary made
By and for us alone

Beatific

In what guise will next we meet?
Will late bloom love
Once more visit our days
Filling nights with passion
Burning more fiercely for it

To be robbed of even a single day
Hour, week or second
Of this joy
This tranquil bliss
Would be tragedy most profound

Across time and space and place
From those lives lived
And those yet to come
I will know you still
I will love you
Always and forever

Reunion

I Cannot Love You Anymore

I cannot love you anymore
Than I do already
I am full and yet
Each hour, each day, each breath
Still more it grows

Even

The scent of you
A tidal surge
Overtaken
Overwhelmed
I would drown

I cannot love you anymore
Than you will let me
Except at peril of my life

Spring

You invade my soul
The way Spring does to Winter
An army
Of hope, color and new life
An army
Of love

Life

The best paths are seldom STRAIGHT or LEVEL . They take you to grand places, quiet places and small places. Sometimes it seems you're not getting anywhere, but if you keep moving, the journey will take you exactly where you need to go. The best paths don't take you to a destination. The best paths are the destination.

Beyond

<u>RISE</u> above the fray. Extend beyond the ordinary, the mundane and the safe. Bring beauty, hope and color to the gray zones. Shine light in the darkness and wield inspiration to vanquish despair.

I am nothing

I am God

I am less than a teardrop

And I am the ocean

I am thought

And I am oblivion

A grain of sand

And the cosmos both

Existence and Void

An Ocean of Tears

I am me
And I am you
As you are us

All of us

I am the light
I am the dark
Without one
There cannot be other

Without you
There can be no me

Distant Shores

When next we meet
On the other side
What will we see there?
Will I gaze across the ocean
Of your endless blue eyes
And rest upon the distant shore
Of this side
This life
This time
This us?

Will we see it for what it was
What it could have been
The truth of it?
Will I feel the connection
The thread
And the driven heated need
To cross that chasm of sea?

At the shore
Me in my small craft
And you in yours

Off to circumnavigate the world
Two reciprocal directions
Hope against hope
We meet in the middle
In that featureless flat expanse
Where sunrise and sunset collide
In birth and death
In love and hope

I Knew

I knew you were gone

I knew
And didn't want to know

I knew
With the return of your favorite shirt
Laundered and folded with the scent of me
Washed down some faraway drain

I knew
In the words you spoke
And those you did not
I knew
1,000 miles away I knew
The war in your soul and the wound in your heart
A conflagration when I held you close
Taking my breath
Consuming you
And ultimately us

I knew
That glorious last morning
Cheeks burnt with scalding tears
Leak from my eyes
Pour forth from the well of my soul

I knew
To lose you was to save you
So this I do from love
Released
My hope
My dream
My salvation in this world
To see you fly again
On magnificent golden wings

I so desperately want you
To breathe again
Live again
Even if that cost, though terrible it be
Is far from me
And my love for you

The Fall

I thought I would die
Of old age
Wrapped in your embrace
Or you in mine
Did you kill me that day?
Or did I do it?

Slow, agonizing and unseen
Unwelcome, unbidden
A thief in the night
To steal your heart and mine
And now I plummet from the heavens
On Icarus' waxen wings
Empty and wide eyed
To the frozen ground below

And now
I die alone

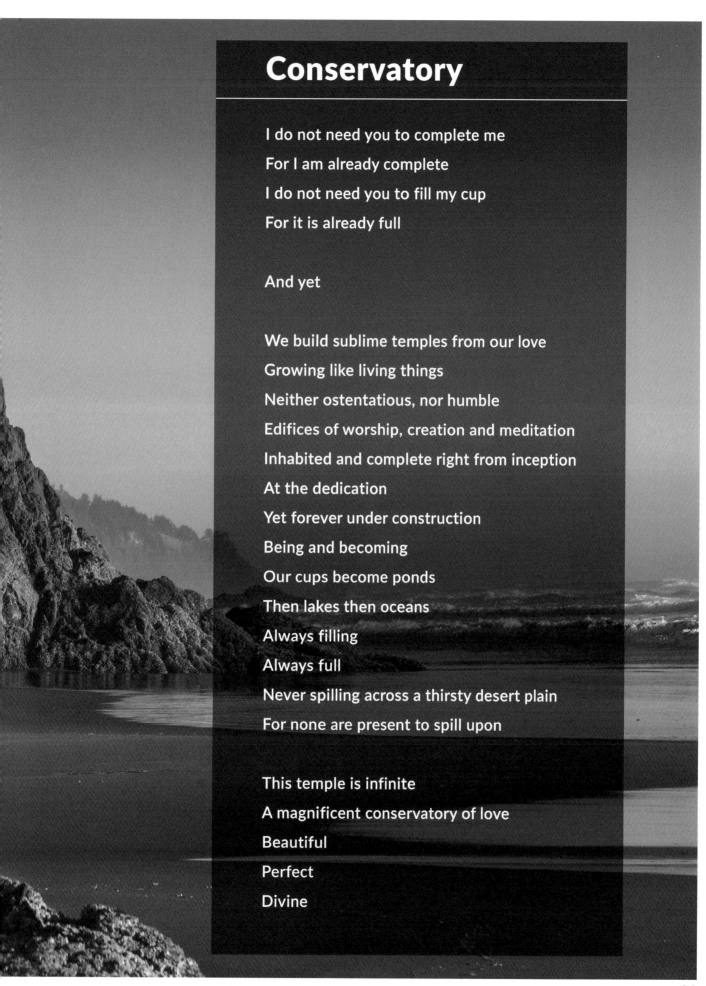

Conservatory

I do not need you to complete me

For I am already complete

I do not need you to fill my cup

For it is already full

And yet

We build sublime temples from our love

Growing like living things

Neither ostentatious, nor humble

Edifices of worship, creation and meditation

Inhabited and complete right from inception

At the dedication

Yet forever under construction

Being and becoming

Our cups become ponds

Then lakes then oceans

Always filling

Always full

Never spilling across a thirsty desert plain

For none are present to spill upon

This temple is infinite

A magnificent conservatory of love

Beautiful

Perfect

Divine

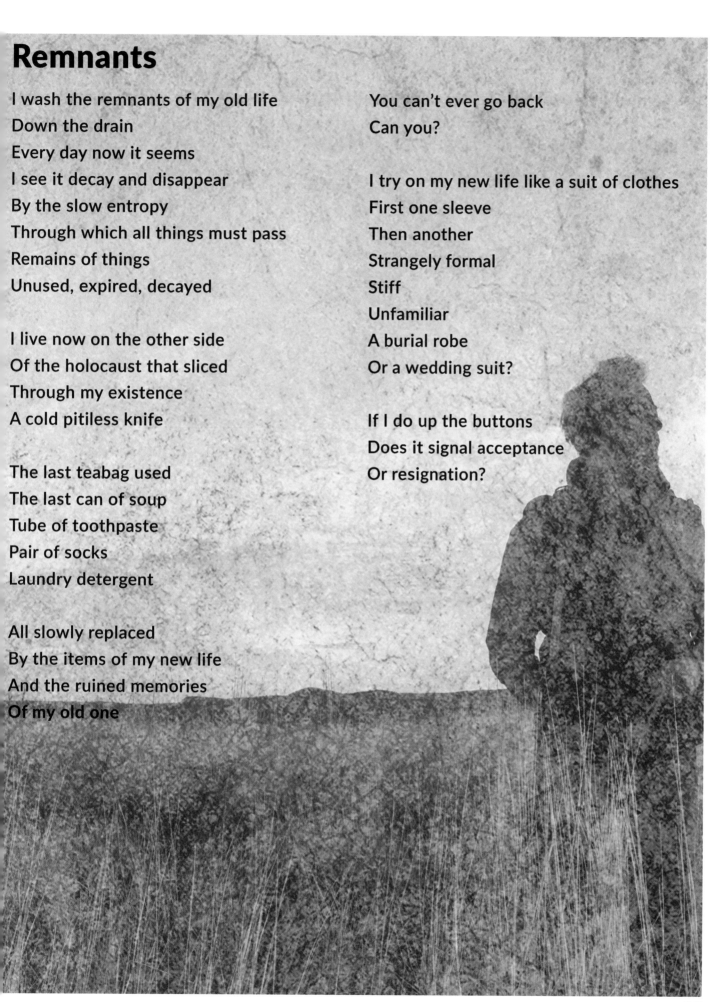

Remnants

I wash the remnants of my old life
Down the drain
Every day now it seems
I see it decay and disappear
By the slow entropy
Through which all things must pass
Remains of things
Unused, expired, decayed

I live now on the other side
Of the holocaust that sliced
Through my existence
A cold pitiless knife

The last teabag used
The last can of soup
Tube of toothpaste
Pair of socks
Laundry detergent

All slowly replaced
By the items of my new life
And the ruined memories
Of my old one

You can't ever go back
Can you?

I try on my new life like a suit of clothes
First one sleeve
Then another
Strangely formal
Stiff
Unfamiliar
A burial robe
Or a wedding suit?

If I do up the buttons
Does it signal acceptance
Or resignation?

Binary Stars

We dance
Binary stars
Each orbiting the other
Two radiant lights
In the vast emptiness of the cosmos
Circling
Just out of reach
Unable to touch
Yet too close to break free
Each trapped by the other's embrace
The pull of gravity
The push of centrifugal force
An exquisite agonizing balance
If I could take your hand
I would embrace you fully
Kiss you passionately
Dance closely
Whisper you my soul
We two together
Shining in the dark
A light for others
A gift for ourselves

Between Worlds

I am lost

In that crack between worlds

Life and death

Day and night

Hope and despair

Seduce me with your love

Let me walk into that beautiful light

Where no shadow is cast

A place devoid

Of thought

Of fear

Of self

A place only for renewal

Rebirth

Guide me there

Take me there

Call to me

Beckon me

Whisper me the way

Reach for my hand

And I will reach back

For Love of Belle

The wound in your soul
A quiet IV drip
Inexorable
Like the mourning tide
Coming in with the dawn
Transformed instead
Into dense wet fog
Dropping rain
And stopping the nascent light
From rightful glorious birth.
Flooding my heart with the song of your pain
I would take this from you
If I could
A small gift purchased
So that you might live again
Laugh again
Love again

If shadows had an opposite
Sculpted from the light of pure love
This then would be
The perfect unblinking avatar
At your side these many years
Feeding you only unconditional love
Asking for naught
But the same
And perhaps a little time
Just a little more time perhaps
Such a simple request yet
Sometimes harder to move
Than any Himalayan giant

Soar in the wind
On powerful wings
Iridescent and gleaming with joy
Carried along on whorls of unseen current
Into a distant place
Of coruscating light and promise

And more difficult to catch
Than any zephyr
How to stop then
This terrible thief
Who has crept in and torn asunder
That warm cozy abode in which we dwell
Stolen
That most precious of all things
Along with it our innocence
And divine inheritance
We cannot prevent the carnage
Nor can we halt this foul predation
For the thief has no master
Obeys no law
And cannot be bribed
We learn then to our horror
Revulsion even
That in point
No crime has even been committed
For we all belong

All of us
To this same master larcenist
We are only loaned out
The way library books and movies
Pass their days
Until that time when we too are returned
Dusty, dog-eared and well used
With torn covers
But we do own our stories - each one
And we take with us
Our friends, lovers and companions
Those we have traveled with
Broken bread with
And flown to the sun and moon and stars with
These live forever
They cannot be taken or excised
By any means, price or coercion
Inseparable
Insoluble
They are us and we are them
We are all part
Of each other and the Universe
Bound together by love
And by loss

Transfiguration

The slow realization
Inevitable shift from love to loss
Extinguishing me
Suffocating me
A candle needs oxygen to burn
The way an osprey needs water and the sky
You are my wind
I cannot fly
Without the wind
Am I Phoenix or ash?

Rebirth

In my darkest despair
Clawing dirt
From a grave of my own device
I called your name
Though knew it not
I prayed your light and warmth
Your breath to guide my way
And come you did
To my aid

My sun

My dazzling beautiful sun
An ocean bloom
Bring me life
Bring me love
Light my way
To rebirth at journey's end

Loss

The last remnants of my soul
Disappear into the dark of night
Like a sigh
Carried off by the breeze
As a whisper
And then I am gone
Toward the distant break of dawn
That may never come
Because I am already too broken
Beyond the repair of this life
Silent and alone

Symbols of Grandeur

I stood upon a monument of man
To himself
Crumbling, alone and dying slowly
Shared fate with mortal creators
And those who would be gods
I watched swirling death
Cold and fluid beneath
Ribs of rusting steel poking obscenely out
From a skin of cracked gray paste
I saw from it a blur of color and shape
Depthless walls in which walked
The past

Gone forever, but lingering on eternity
Tireless, flying on to forever
A window lent me sight
For my own brief span
And I too saw myself
A crumbling ruin
Too soon vanquished
And gone
A monument to myself
For all of time

Mirrors

I saw myself in a mirror of time today
The clear reflection in a small face
With eyes that sparkled, laughed, cried
Were curious and new
All at once

I saw myself with the Universe at my feet
On a road of golden doors
Going to undiscovered destiny
With my eyes open and untarnished and alive
In a hurry

I saw myself in a mirror of time today
A cracked image of weathered age
With a hundred false eyes clouded
By time and a fading sense of immortality
Made clear by the imminence of my own end

I stood upon a road
Its surface worn ragged and lined
End to end with unopened doors
And a thousand laughing mirrors
I saw a past that never was

And I wept

I saw myself in a mirror of time today
With vanishing clarity and already exhausted
By an illusion of heat from a noonday sun
I traveled more slowly now
Thinking of morning
Hopeful and cool and calm

There were already weeds along my path
Left twisted and strewn
By other travelers sharing the road
I ignored those left in my own wake
Interested in only the bright doors now
Cursing myself silently

The Arrow

I was born a million years ago
And I died yesterday
I was born a thousand years from now
And I died tomorrow
I have always lived
Knowing of my birth
Blind to my death
Time is not a unilateral flow
I am not immortal
As assured of death as of birth
It has already happened
It has yet to take place
It has always been thus

Temporal Tides

The beginning of time was a collision with motion

The void would shatter

Should the tick of time's hand mark its place

Nothing cannot be measured by the temporal

The silent motion of event

Its own witness and envelope

Should nothing intercede the infinite

And motion's flow

Cease for the space of the void's timeless rule

There would be no gap

Since nothing cannot be measured

The trick lies in motion's own beginning

And nothing's end

Returning Home

Returning home
Alone
With a head of bristling posibility
Unity flowing without key
Abandoned illusions
Which for so long held him fooled
Vanished when a face of weathered age
Was hewn from the visage of a youth
Still there
Not yet usurped by the elements
But only by the self
The sea
Gently caressed his soul
While blithely pounding sinew to a pulp
For years
No longer an enemy to be fought
Subdued
Now simply understood
Cared for and sailed on
Exhilarating
As with imagination

Returning home
The still water no longer reflected the image
He strove so hard to create
From the bottomless unfathomable blackness
And gently rippling waves
He knew it was gone, never to return
But he did not mourn for it
As once he did when first had lost it

Returning home
From a voyage that would end
Only with his own
He remembered a contrived beginning
But couldn't fully recollect exactly
When it all began
It didn't matter really
It was only a point in time
Left smudged and blurry
On the fragile film of his mind

Returning home

He yearned only for the place, the time
That thrust itself upon him
Calling his name and itself
Home
But for all its allure
It had the clarity and solidity
Of a single wave, chosen at random
From a vantage point at the helm of his boat
Followed recklessly across the expanse of sea
Through storms and ports and good times
Til it was lost in all respects
Save as cause, as purpose

Returning home

He followed the wave
He knew
Returning home
He would find only himself
Returning home

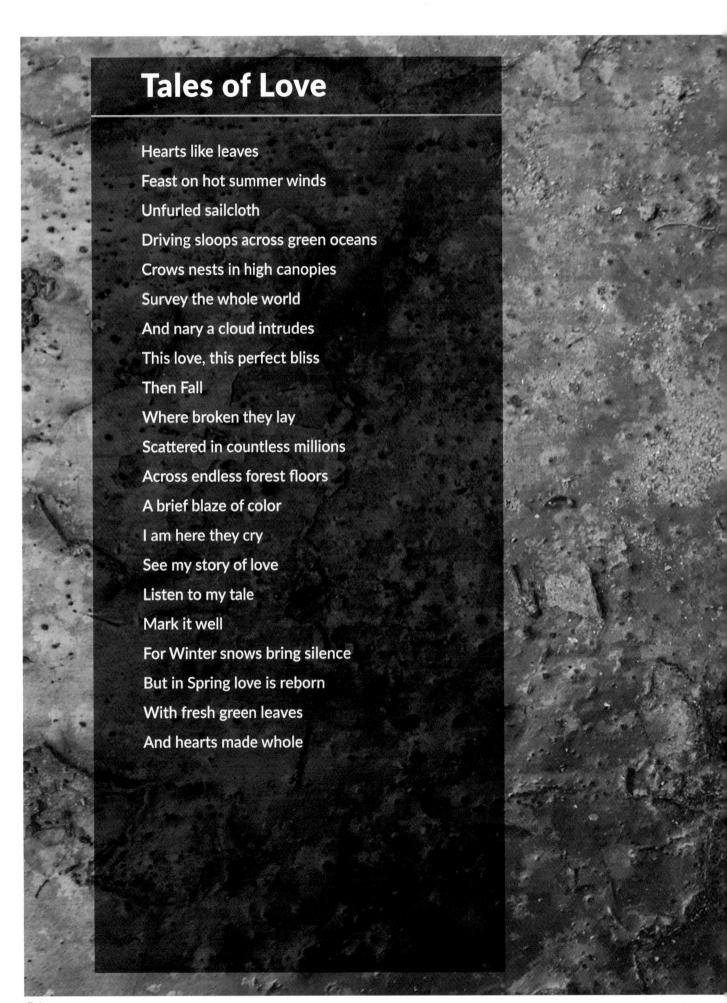

Tales of Love

Hearts like leaves

Feast on hot summer winds

Unfurled sailcloth

Driving sloops across green oceans

Crows nests in high canopies

Survey the whole world

And nary a cloud intrudes

This love, this perfect bliss

Then Fall

Where broken they lay

Scattered in countless millions

Across endless forest floors

A brief blaze of color

I am here they cry

See my story of love

Listen to my tale

Mark it well

For Winter snows bring silence

But in Spring love is reborn

With fresh green leaves

And hearts made whole

Flight to Nowhere

I have wings
But will not fly
So here I cling
Afraid to die

Beyond the Sky

The sky isn't the limit
It is only the beginning
Look up
Reach out
We already live there
Now where to from here?

Beyond Lost Horizons

Out beyond the rim of reasonable
Where cold and isolation claim all things
Where even oxygen gasps for breath
Where liquid made brittle
Becomes sculptural castles and otherworld jewels
Beautiful and terrible in equal measure both

There is life

In regions where the dawn brings no sun
Each step a gaping chasm cross
Where void fills all existence with nothing

There is hope

In vast seas where towering waves blot out stars
Lands where creatures fierce and endless would
consume all flesh
Through expansive skies where still the wingless
would soar
For those fools who would ascend
Oceans of polished vertical granite armed
Only with fingers and toes yet

There is courage

In places where history is razed and memory now
Too terrible to contemplate or rescue
Where connection lays burnt and turned to ash
For those kept in dungeons deep
Where tufts of stale bread and foul water a feast
would make

There is love

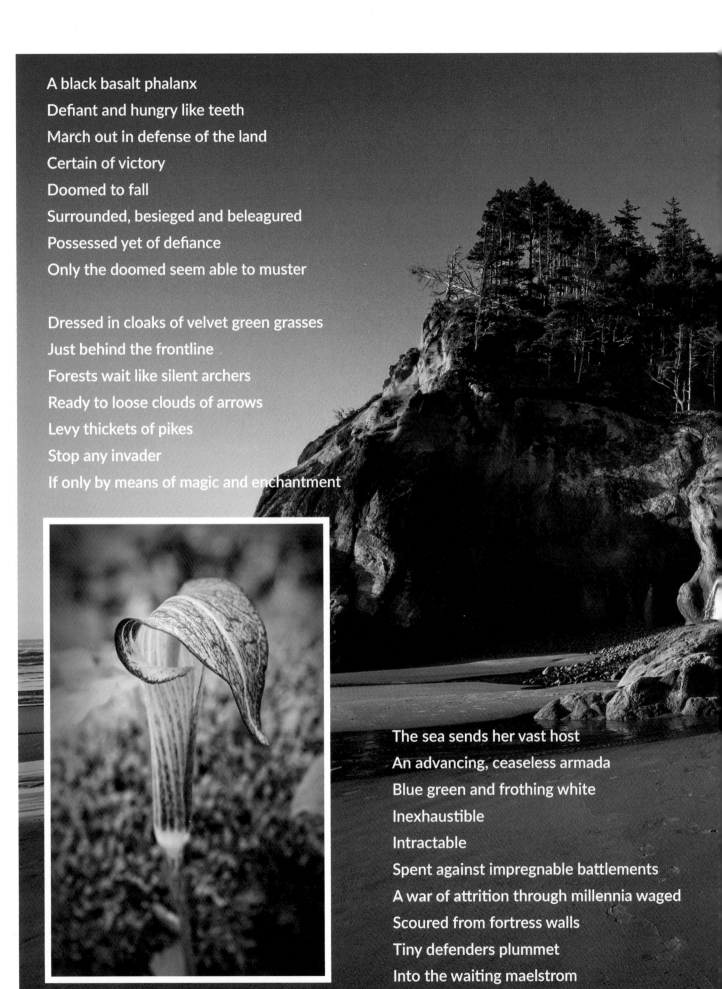

A black basalt phalanx
Defiant and hungry like teeth
March out in defense of the land
Certain of victory
Doomed to fall
Surrounded, besieged and beleaguered
Possessed yet of defiance
Only the doomed seem able to muster

Dressed in cloaks of velvet green grasses
Just behind the frontline
Forests wait like silent archers
Ready to loose clouds of arrows
Levy thickets of pikes
Stop any invader
If only by means of magic and enchantment

The sea sends her vast host
An advancing, ceaseless armada
Blue green and frothing white
Inexhaustible
Intractable
Spent against impregnable battlements
A war of attrition through millennia waged
Scoured from fortress walls
Tiny defenders plummet
Into the waiting maelstrom

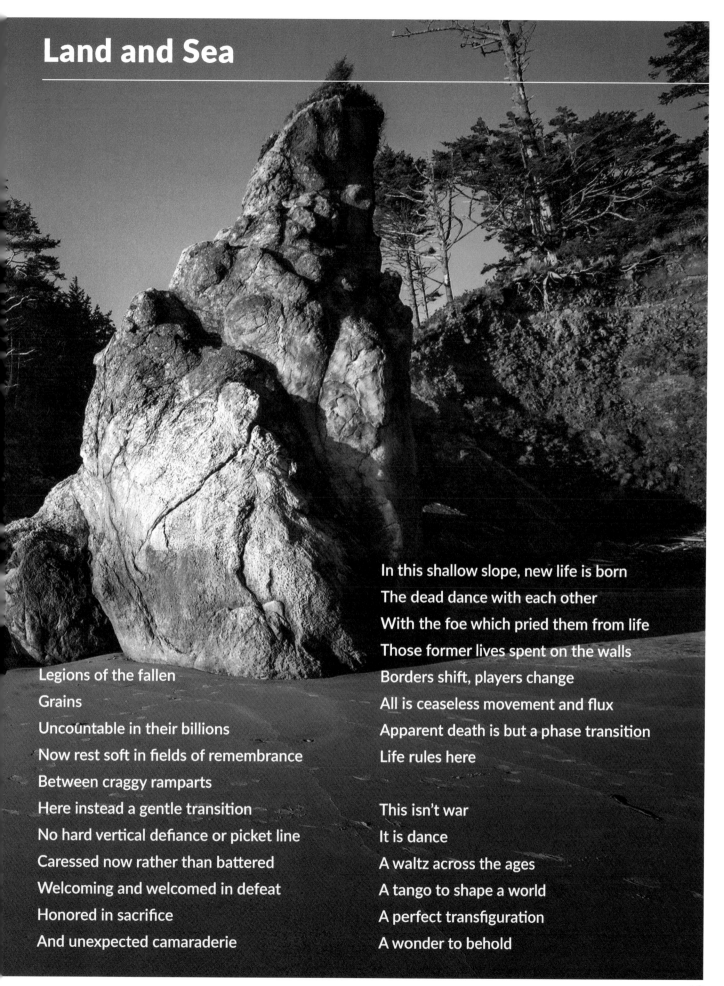

Land and Sea

In this shallow slope, new life is born
The dead dance with each other
With the foe which pried them from life
Those former lives spent on the walls

Legions of the fallen
Grains
Uncountable in their billions
Now rest soft in fields of remembrance
Between craggy ramparts
Here instead a gentle transition
No hard vertical defiance or picket line
Caressed now rather than battered
Welcoming and welcomed in defeat
Honored in sacrifice
And unexpected camaraderie

Borders shift, players change
All is ceaseless movement and flux
Apparent death is but a phase transition
Life rules here

This isn't war
It is dance
A waltz across the ages
A tango to shape a world
A perfect transfiguration
A wonder to behold

Seeds of New Life

Whether by choice or design
Some are engulfed by darkness
Cast into shadowed places
Where eyes cannot see
And there are no paths to follow
Where hope is the only succor

A journey from which egress may not be found
Hard won when it is
Sunlight fades and the day ends
Waiting for a new one to be born

Not all seeds sown in the fall
Find their way through winter
Sometimes a chrysalis is only a tomb
But sometimes it is not
Survivors emerge transformed
From promise and hope and effort
To kiss patterned skies
Wearing multi-colored cloaks with names
Tulip, Rose, Orchid, Calathea, Lotus...
You and me

Flavors of vivid imagination made real
Ready to dance with bees
Feast on warm sunshine
Bathe in the great cycle of life
Donate sublime beauty in return only
For love, appreciation and hearts
Made light
Pure from experience
Simply being is enough
Grateful to breathe the air
To love and be loved
The only true coin

CPSIA information can be obtained at www.ICGtesting.com
Printed in the USA
LVIW01n0838100418
572168LV00005B/3